AI for Young Entrepreneurs

Building Smart Businesses with Artificial Intelligence

Amaara Verma & Abeer Verma

Fusion Books

Publisher	**:**	**Fusion Books** X-30, Okhla Industrial Area, Phase-II New Delhi-110020
Phone	:	011- 40712200
E-mail	:	wecare@diamondbooks.in
Website	:	www.diamondbooks.in
Edition	:	2026

AUTHOR'S NOTE

Entrepreneurship no longer requires massive capital or a big team. It requires clarity, creativity — and intelligent use of Artificial Intelligence.

As students exploring AI tools, we realized something powerful:
AI is not just helping people learn — it's helping them build.
Abeer was fascinated by how AI can automate, analyze, and accelerate business tasks.

Amaara kept asking deeper questions — How should AI be used in business? Where do we draw ethical boundaries? How do we build trust while using smart tools?
This book brings both perspectives together.

If you have ever wondered:

- Can I start a business as a student?
- Can AI reduce my startup costs?
- How do I automate responsibly?
- What skills will matter in an AI-driven economy?

Then this book is for you.
AI does not replace entrepreneurs.
It empowers thoughtful ones.
Let's build smart — and build responsibly.

— Abeer & Amaara

PREFACE

Why AI Changes Entrepreneurship Forever
The rules of business are changing faster than ever.

Artificial Intelligence has transformed how companies:
• Analyze customers
• Predict trends
• Automate operations
• Personalize marketing
• Manage finances
• Build digital products
What once required large teams and expensive infrastructure can now be done with smart AI tools and strategic thinking.

This creates an extraordinary opportunity for young entrepreneurs. You no longer need to wait for adulthood to start building. With the right understanding of AI, **even students can:**
• Launch digital services
• Create content-driven businesses
• Design AI-assisted products
• Build data-driven solutions
• Optimize operations efficiently

This book simplifies AI for business — step by step.
It focuses not on complex coding, but on:
• Identifying real-world problems
• Using AI tools wisely
• Building ethical ventures
• Thinking strategically
• Managing risk
• Understanding future-ready business models
Entrepreneurship today is not just about ideas.
It's about intelligent execution.
And AI is the ultimate execution partner.

FOREWORD

We are witnessing the birth of a new entrepreneurial era.
In previous decades, capital, infrastructure, and manpower were the primary drivers of business success. Today, intelligence — both human and artificial — plays a defining role.

Artificial Intelligence has democratized opportunity.

Young founders now have access to tools that:
• Analyze markets
• Automate customer support
• Generate branding assets
• Optimize logistics
• Improve decision-making

AI for Young Entrepreneurs captures this transformation in a way that speaks directly to the next generation.

By combining technical curiosity with critical thinking, Abeer and Amaara Verma present a practical guide to building intelligent businesses responsibly.

This book does not glorify AI blindly.
It encourages thoughtful, ethical innovation.
In an age where technology evolves daily, young entrepreneurs who understand AI will not just participate in the future — they will shape it.

The future of business is intelligent.
The future of intelligence is human-led.

INDEX

Chapter 1

What is AI – And Why Every Entrepreneur Needs It

Introduction: The Rise of Smart Work

Imagine having a super-intelligent assistant who never sleeps, always listens, understands your business needs, and gives you instant solutions—whether it's writing a product description, answering a customer query, creating a logo, or analyzing sales trends. This assistant doesn't need lunch breaks, salaries, or coffee. Sounds magical? Welcome to the world of Artificial Intelligence, or AI.

In this chapter, we will understand what AI really is, how it works, and why it's the ultimate business ally for today's entrepreneurs—especially students, solopreneurs, and small business owners.

What is AI? (Defining the Basics)

Artificial Intelligence, or AI, is the ability of machines—like computers and software—to think, learn, and make decisions like humans. Just like your brain learns from experience, AI systems learn from data and patterns. They observe, calculate, and improve their performance over time.

There are many types of AI, and here are a few key terms every entrepreneur should know:

Key Terms Simplified:

- **AI (Artificial Intelligence):** Technology that mimics human thinking and decision-making.
- **Machine Learning (ML):** A part of AI where machines learn from data without being explicitly programmed.
- **Natural Language Processing (NLP):** AI's ability to understand and respond to human language (like what Siri or Alexa do).
- **Generative AI:** A type of AI that can create something new—like text, images, or videos. Tools like ChatGPT or DALL·E use generative AI.
- **Automation:** Letting AI handle repetitive tasks automatically, like sending invoices or scheduling meetings.

The 5Ws of AI for Entrepreneurs

Let's break it down using the 5Ws framework to understand the value of AI in business:

1. What is AI in Business?

AI in business refers to using smart technology tools to handle tasks like:

- Writing content
- Managing customer service
- Automating accounting
- Creating designs
- Making decisions based on data

It's not about robots taking over your job—it's about boosting your superpowers as a founder.

2. Why Use AI?

Because it helps you:

- **Save time** – AI can write a blog post in 5 minutes.
- **Cut costs** – No need to hire separate teams for every task.
- **Work faster** – AI never takes a break.
- **Think smarter** – Use data to make informed business decisions.
- **Compete better** – Small businesses can now compete with big companies.

Example: A high school student running a handmade soap business uses Canva AI to design packaging, ChatGPT to write product descriptions, and Zapier to automate Instagram posting. She's doing the work of five people—by herself!

3. When Should You Use AI?

Any time you want to:

- Boost productivity
- Solve a problem
- Save effort on repetitive work
- Make faster decisions
- Launch quicker

Use AI when you need a helping hand but don't have the time, team, or budget to do everything manually.

Tip: Don't wait for things to become perfect. Start with AI tools that solve one small problem—like summarizing notes, creating a to-do list, or replying to customer emails.

4. Who is Using AI?

From small café owners to tech CEOs, everyone is using AI:

- Startups use AI for branding, pitch decks, and hiring.
- Teachers use AI to plan lessons.
- Students use AI to take notes or build project ideas.
- Retailers use AI for inventory tracking and order automation.
- Social media influencers use AI to edit videos and generate captions.

Fun Fact: 8 out of 10 small businesses in the U.S. say AI helps them grow faster. In India, tools like WhatsApp Business and Zoho AI are helping kirana stores and tutors scale like pros.

5. Where to Start With AI?

Start with your biggest pain point. Ask:

- Do I spend too much time replying to emails?
- Is designing taking me forever?
- Do I find it hard to explain my product?

Then pick an AI tool for that specific task. Some beginner-friendly **tools:**

- **ChatGPT** – Writing, summaries, emails
- **Canva** – Posters, social media, branding
- **Fireflies.ai** – Meeting transcription
- **Tome** – Beautiful AI presentations

We'll cover 100+ such tools in this book, categorized by use.

Real Business Examples Using AI

Let's look at how big brands and small businesses alike use AI:

Netflix

Uses AI to analyze what you watch and suggest shows. That same tech can be used by entrepreneurs to understand what their customers want.

Amazon
Uses AI in delivery planning, product recommendations, and even pricing. Students can use similar tools (like Shopify + AI plugins) for their online stores.

Swiggy
Uses AI for route optimization, chatbot ordering, and customer queries. Small cafés and cloud kitchens now use tools like Quickchat for their WhatsApp orders.

You don't have to be a tech genius. You just need to know what AI can do—and let it work for you.

How AI Levels the Playing Field for Youth Entrepreneurs

Before AI, businesses needed:
- Designers for branding
- Writers for blogs
- Admins for scheduling
- Analysts for reports

Now with AI, a solo founder or a school team can do all of this and more, at almost zero cost.

Case Study:
Ria, a 17-year-old student, launched a custom T-shirt brand from her hostel.

She used:
- Looka for logo
- Durable to build her website
- Writesonic for product descriptions
- Trello + Butler AI to manage orders

In 3 months, she made 40,000 in profit without hiring anyone.

Common Areas Where AI Helps in Business

Area	AI Use-Cases
Marketing	Create ads, write posts, design banners
Content	Write blogs, newsletters, product descriptions
Sales	Automate email follow-ups, create offers
Customer Service	Answer queries with chatbots, collect feedback
Admin	Schedule meetings, manage tasks, send invoices
Finance	Budgeting, tax estimates, price planning
Research	Gather insights, summarize market reports
Product Dev	Brainstorm ideas, plan features, prototype with no-code AI tools

Myths About AI – Busted!

× **"AI will take all our jobs."**

✓ **Truth:** AI assists you. It doesn't replace your creativity, empathy, or leadership.

× **"You need to be a programmer to use AI."**

✓ **Truth:** Most tools today are no-code and very beginner-friendly.

× **"Only big businesses benefit from AI."**

✓ **Truth:** In fact, AI benefits small businesses and students the most—because it saves time, money, and effort.

Learning AI is Like Learning Excel in the 90s

Back then, businesses that didn't learn Excel were left behind. Today, it's AI. If you don't learn how to use it, you'll be stuck doing things manually while your competition zips ahead.

But if you learn even basic tools like:
• ChatGPT for writing
• Canva for design
• Zapier for automation

...you'll be 10x faster, more professional, and more competitive—even as a teenager.

Activity: AI Self-Check

Answer these for yourself:
1. What is one task I do daily that AI could help with?
2. Have I ever used a chatbot? What was the experience?
3. Which tool in this chapter would I like to try first?
4. What business idea could I test using only AI tools?

Try This: Your First AI Productivity Test

Go to https://chat.openai.com
Ask: "Write a product description for a handmade clay pen holder."

Then go to https://canva.com
Use AI design suggestions to make a matching product poster.

You just built content + marketing in 10 minutes!

Founder's Insight

Abeer's Take
AI reduces operational friction. The faster your systems run, the more time you have to innovate.
Amaara's Take
But speed without direction is dangerous. First define the problem clearly — then apply AI.

Chapter Summary

• AI = smart tools that mimic human thinking to boost productivity, creativity, and decision-making.
• The 5Ws framework helps you understand AI from a business lens.
• AI helps solo entrepreneurs, students, and SMEs do more with less.
• You don't need to be a tech expert—just start with one small use.
• In the age of AI, learning to use tools is your new superpower.

Chapter 2

AI for Solo Hustlers, Startups & SMEs

How Small Teams Can Do Big Things with Smart Tech

The Power of One – Running a Business Without a Big Team

Running a business used to mean managing people, renting office space, and working long hours. But now, with AI, even a solo founder or a small team can handle tasks that once needed a full department. This is the age of lean, smart entrepreneurship.

Whether you're:
- A teenager selling art online,
- A tuition teacher expanding digitally,
- A college student launching a startup, or
- A small business owner with 3 employees...

AI is your secret weapon to do more with less.

In this chapter, we explore how AI tools level the playing field for solo hustlers, student entrepreneurs, and SMEs (Small and Medium Enterprises).

Why AI is a Solo Entrepreneur's Best Friend

Solopreneurs and micro-teams face these common challenges:

- Too much to do, not enough time
- Limited budget to hire people
- No technical or marketing expertise
- Need to move fast and try new ideas

AI solves all of these by:

- Automating repetitive tasks
- Acting as your virtual assistant, designer, writer, and planner
- Helping you compete with larger players

Key Insight: With AI, even one person can operate like a team of five.

Let's Break It Down: What Can AI Do for You?

Productivity Hacks

- Use Reclaim.ai to automatically block time for important tasks
- Use Motion to auto-schedule meetings and work blocks
- Use Notion AI to plan your week or write your goals

Cost-Cutting

- Replace expensive software with free/low-cost AI tools
- Save on hiring by using AI to write content, design graphics, and handle customer queries
- Use Zapier to link apps together so you don't need a developer

Customer Insight

- Use Perplexity AI to research what your customers care about
- Analyze feedback using ChatGPT to summarize and extract trends

• Use Google Forms + AI analysis tools to generate reports and plan improvements

Use-Cases for Solopreneurs & Startups

Use-Case	AI Tool	Impact
Writing social media captions	ChatGPT, Jasper	Save hours and improve quality
Designing product brochures	Canva, Looka	DIY branding without hiring a designer
Managing bookings & tasks	ClickUp AI, Trello + Butler	Organize your week like a pro
Sending invoices	QuickBooks AI, Fincent	Automate accounting in minutes
Creating product explainer videos	Lumen5, Runway ML	Share ideas visually on YouTube or Instagram
Making sales presentations	Beautiful.ai, Tome	Pitch like a startup founder in Silicon Valley
Handling customer queries	Quickchat, ChatSpot	Available 24/7 to serve customers

Real-Life Examples: Small Effort, Big Results

Example 1: The Schoolbag Startup
Naman, a 12th-grade student in Bengaluru, started a brand selling eco-friendly school bags.

Here's how he used AI:
• **Product Research:** Used Perplexity to learn what students want in a bag
• **Logo + Brand Kit**: Designed in Canva Pro with AI templates

• **Product Video:** Made with Lumen5 using customer testimonials
• **Customer Support:** Handled via a WhatsApp bot built on Quickchat

He received over 350 pre-orders within 2 months—all while studying for board exams.

Example 2: The Freelance Artist

Nidhi, a college student and illustrator, wanted to grow her Instagram art page into a business.

She used:
• ChatGPT to write captions and art descriptions
• Canva AI to make carousel posts
• Fireflies.ai to record and summarize client calls
• Zapier to automate email responses when someone filled a form on her website

Result? She doubled her followers, increased orders, and now teaches art on Zoom—managing it all solo with AI tools.

For Small Teams and SMEs: Multiply Impact Without Hiring Big

If you're a team of 2–10 people, AI helps divide and conquer:
• Let AI handle the repetitive grunt work
• Let humans focus on creativity, strategy, and relationships

Team Task Mapping with AI:

Role	AI Assistant
Founder	ChatGPT for planning and emails
Designer	Canva for templates, Midjourney for visuals

Sales Lead	ChatSpot for lead gen, CRM automation
Admin	Reclaim for scheduling, Zapier for tasks
Support Agent	Quickchat for 24/7 query handling

Tool Tip: Even if your team has no technical background, tools like Durable (instant website builder) and Writesonic (AI content creator) make it easy to launch and grow online.

Common Questions Students Ask About AI for Startups

? "Can I run a real business using only AI?"

✓ Yes. Many creators, coaches, artists, and freelancers use 100% AI-powered workflows.

? "What if I mess up while using a tool?"

✓ That's okay! Most AI tools are forgiving. You can undo, retry, or edit.

? "Is it expensive to use AI?"

✓ Most tools have free versions or student plans. You can start with 0.

Top 10 AI Tools for Solo Hustlers to Try First

Tool	What It Does	Link
ChatGPT	Writing, emails, scripts	chat.openai.com
Canva	Graphics, videos, logos	canva.com
Fireflies.ai	Meeting transcription	fireflies.ai
Durable	Build websites in 30 seconds	durable.co

Trello + Butler	Task planning with AI automations	trello.com
Jasper AI	Social media, ad copywriting	jasper.ai
Notion AI	Smart notes, documents, planners	notion.so
Looka	Branding kits and logos	looka.com
Reclaim	Calendar automation	reclaim.ai
Quickchat	AI chatbot for customer service	quickchat.ai

What Makes AI So Powerful for Student Startups?

- No need to hire or outsource—AI is your smart teammate
- Test ideas quickly—build MVPs or pitch decks overnight
- Automate boring stuff—focus your time on learning or selling
- Look professional—designs, copy, branding all in minutes
- Learn real-world business skills—while still in school or college

NEP 2020 Goal Achieved: Using AI tools helps students develop 21st-century skills like digital literacy, problem-solving, and entrepreneurship.

Activity: AI in My Business Plan

Use this format to brainstorm your startup:
Business Idea: _______________
Problem it solves: _______________

What I can use AI for:
- Content: ____________________
- Design: ____________________
- Customer help: _______________
- Website/Tech: _______________

Tool I will start with first: _______________

Quick Win Challenge

Can you set up a 3-step business funnel in 1 day?
1. Use Durable to create a website
2. Use ChatGPT to write product text
3. Use Quickchat to add a chatbot for queries

If yes—you've launched a startup using AI in 24 hours!

Founder's Insight

Abeer's Take
Before building a product, test ideas using AI tools for surveys, keyword research, and competitor analysis.
Amaara's Take
Don't build what AI can already generate for free. Build what combines human creativity with AI efficiency.

Chapter Summary

• Solopreneurs and small teams can use AI to run and scale their business affordably.
• AI handles tasks like design, content, scheduling, and support.
• You don't need money or a tech background to start—just the right tools and mindset.
• Real student examples prove that AI startups are already here.
• Start small: pick one tool, solve one task, and grow from there.

Chapter 3

Meet Your AI Agents & Assistants

Your Smart Digital Teammates for Everyday Business Tasks

Introduction: AI Isn't Just a Tool – It's a Teammate

Imagine having an assistant who never sleeps, replies instantly, remembers everything, learns fast, and can do everything from answering emails to summarizing meetings, designing posts, and handling bookings. The good news? You already have access to them.

They're called AI agents and assistants.

This chapter introduces you to the powerful world of digital agents—the invisible workers who help businesses operate faster, smarter, and cheaper. Whether you're a student startup founder or a growing SME, AI agents are your always-on allies.

What is an AI Agent or Assistant?

An AI agent is a computer program or system that can:

- Sense what's happening (read input),
- Think or plan based on goals,
- Act by performing tasks.

In simple words, they behave like mini-employees with limited but smart intelligence, trained to handle specific duties.

Think of them like:

- A receptionist who answers all your customer chats
- A marketing intern who writes captions for you
- A virtual secretary who schedules meetings

The difference? These agents are software-powered, require no physical presence, and work 24/7.

Types of AI Agents You'll Meet in Business

Let's meet the four main types of AI-powered agents and assistants:

1. Chatbots

- These are the most common AI agents.
- They simulate human conversation using Natural Language Processing (NLP).
- Used for customer support, lead generation, FAQs, onboarding, and surveys.

Popular Tools:

- Quickchat.ai
- ChatSpot by HubSpot
- Kuki AI
- Tidio

Real Example:

A tuition teacher adds a chatbot on their WhatsApp Business account. It answers students' common queries like "When is the next class?" or "How do I pay fees?"

2. Virtual Assistants

- These are like personal secretaries.
- They can schedule meetings, remind you of tasks, fetch informa tion, and even write emails.
- Some assistants live inside apps like Google Assistant, Siri, or Reclaim AI.

Popular Tools:

- Motion (plans your day intelligently)
- Reclaim.ai (calendar optimizer)
- Microsoft 365 Copilot
- Notion AI

Real Example:

A student entrepreneur uses Reclaim to automatically block time for focused work and reschedules meetings based on urgency.

3. Creative Agents

- These are tools that generate content—text, images, videos, presen tations, and more.
- They use Generative AI to create new outputs from prompts.

Popular Tools:

- ChatGPT (text assistant)
- Midjourney (AI art)
- DALL·E (image creation)
- Tome (smart presentations)

Real Example:

An NGO founder asks ChatGPT to write an email to potential donors,

Midjourney to create a poster, and Tome to build the pitch deck.

4. Browser & Workflow Agents

- These agents act in the background and perform actions across websites.
- They can extract data, autofill forms, send files, or trigger workflows.

Popular Tools:

- Harpa AI (web scraping + browsing)
- AIrops (workflow automation)
- Zapier AI Agents
- n8n (low-code automation)

Real Example:

A small food delivery business uses Zapier to auto-send SMS when an order form is filled on their website.

Active vs Passive Agents: What's the Difference?

Agent Type	Active	Passive
Definition	Takes initiative, plans and executes	Responds only when asked
Example	Motion rearranging your schedule	ChatGPT answering your question
Analogy	A proactive assistant	A responsive helper

You can mix both types to build a smart team:

- Use Reclaim to manage your day (active)
- Use Claude or ChatGPT to write plans (passive)

How Do These Agents Think? The Agent Loop

Most AI agents work through a simple loop:

1. **Sense:** Read or hear what you want

2. **Plan:** Decide what action is needed
3. **Act:** Do the task (e.g., write, design, reply)
4. **Learn:** Improve for next time (some tools have memory)

Example:
You ask your AI assistant: "Schedule a call with Raj next Friday afternoon."

It will:
• Check your calendar (Sense)
• Find a time that works (Plan)
• Send the invite (Act)
• Note that you prefer Friday PM for meetings (Learn)

Prompting: How to Talk to AI Agents Like a Pro

AI agents respond better to clear, specific instructions, also known as prompts.

Prompting Tips:
• Be clear: "Write a 100-word caption for Instagram"
• Give context: "My startup sells handmade soaps"
• Ask for structure: "Make it bullet points"
• Request tone: "Make it friendly and fun"

Try This:

Open ChatGPT and prompt:

"Act as a customer service agent for a shoe brand. Write a polite response to a late delivery."

See how it replies—then refine it!

Tools That Act Like Smart Teammates

Function	AI Agent / Tool	What It Does
Social media posts	Copy.ai, Jasper	Writes captions and blogs
Meeting notes	Fireflies, Tactiq	Records and summarizes calls
Website builder	Durable, Wix ADI	Creates entire website with AI
Email replies	ChatGPT, Microsoft Copilot	Writes responses in your tone
Calendar planner	Reclaim, Motion	Arranges your week automatically
Forms + responses	Typeform + VideoAsk	Collects info with smart forms and video bots

Real Case: The One-Woman PR Agency

Shruti, 23, runs a PR firm alone. Here's her AI-powered team:

- **ChatGPT** – Client proposals
- **Jasper** – Press releases
- **Canva AI** – Media kits
- **Fireflies.ai** – Summarize Zoom calls
- **Zapier** – Automate feedback form > Google Sheets
- **Harpa AI** – Track mentions online

Result: She's closing 1 lakh/month in projects, managing 6 clients—without hiring a single person.

Where to Place AI Agents in Your Startup or SME

Area	Agent Tool Example
Sales	ChatSpot, Drift
Marketing	Writesonic, Jasper
Design	Canva AI, Midjourney
Admin	Reclaim, Motion
Customer Support	Kuki, Quickchat
Data	Claude, ChatGPT, PromptLoop
Research	Perplexity, Consensus, NotebookLM

Mix and match based on your business size and goal.

How Smart Are These Agents Really?

While AI agents are powerful, remember:

- They can generate smart responses—but may make errors.
- They don't have emotions or intuition like humans.
- They follow patterns, not understanding.

That's why you must review outputs, use your judgment, and never copy-paste blindly.

The Human-AI Team: Best of Both Worlds

AI Does Best	You Do Best
Repetition	Creativity & vision
Data handling	Emotional intelligence
Speed	Strategy & decision-making
Consistency	Empathy & storytelling

When you use AI as a co-pilot, you unlock the real power of smart business.

Mini Exercise: Design Your AI Agent Workflow

Try filling this out for your startup:

Task: ____________________________
Agent I will try: _________________
Expected result: _________________
Next action if it works: __________

Chapter Summary

• AI agents are smart digital workers that help you automate, respond, create, and plan.
• There are many types: chatbots, assistants, creative agents, workflow bots.
• You can start using them even as a student or solo entrepreneur—no coding required.
• Prompting well is the key to getting better outputs.
• Use AI agents to reduce workload, not remove human thinking.
• They're your teammates, not your replacements.

Chapter 4

Marketing & Branding with AI

Grow Your Business and Stand Out—Faster, Smarter, Cheaper

Introduction: The Smart Way to Market Your Brand

Marketing used to take weeks of planning, creative brainstorming, graphic designing, and back-and-forth edits. Now, with AI, you can launch a campaign in minutes—even if you're just starting out or don't have a marketing team.

In this chapter, we'll explore how AI tools can help you market your business, build your brand identity, and connect with your audience using zero-code, low-cost solutions.
Whether you're a student running a side hustle, a freelancer looking to grow, or a small business owner aiming to compete with big brands—AI puts the power of professional marketing in your hands.

Why Marketing Matters – Especially for Startups & SMEs

• No matter how great your product is, if people don't know about it, it won't sell.
• Branding is your identity; marketing is how you show it to the world.

But marketing requires:
• Creative ideas
• Catchy content
• Eye-catching visuals
• Strategic thinking

And that's where AI becomes your marketing team—designing, writing, planning, and optimizing in real-time.

What Can AI Help You Do in Marketing & Branding?

Marketing Task	AI Can Help You...
Social media posts	Write, design, and schedule content
Ad copy	Generate sales-driven copy in seconds
Brand name/logo	Suggest unique names, create logos and color palettes
Product descriptions	Write SEO-friendly descriptions for websites or Amazon
Presentation decks	Build branded slides and investor decks automatically
Email marketing	Craft campaigns, auto-personalize, and analyze results
Video content	Create explainer videos or product reels with AI

Fun Fact: Many viral Instagram ads today are created using AI—from idea to edit—in under 30 minutes.

Top AI Tools for Marketing & Branding

Here's your AI marketing toolkit you can start using right away:

Text + Content Creation Tools

• Copy.ai – Write ads, slogans, taglines, emails, and blog posts.
• Jasper AI – Tailored marketing copy, sales emails, and social media captions.
• Writesonic – Affordable writing assistant for students and startups.

Example Prompt in Copy.ai:

"Write a catchy Instagram caption for a handmade candle brand launching a new winter scent."

Design & Visual Identity Tools

• Canva (with AI features) – Create Instagram posts, YouTube thumbnails, posters, and flyers.
• Looka – Generate brand kits (logo, fonts, colors) in minutes.
• Brandmark – AI logo designer for modern, minimalistic branding.

Try This:

Use Looka.com to design a brand identity by entering your business name and industry. It gives you a full kit in under 10 minutes.

Email & Campaign Automation Tools

• MailerLite with AI – Design email campaigns with subject line suggestions.
• Sendinblue AI Assistant – Create engaging email templates.
• HubSpot's ChatSpot AI – Combines CRM, sales, and email writing.

Example Use:

Ask ChatGPT: "Write a welcome email for new customers of my

online art store."
Use that in MailerLite to set up an automated welcome campaign.

AI for Videos, Ads & Reels
- Pictory – Turn blog posts or scripts into social media videos.
- Lumen5 – Create explainer or promo videos with stock visuals and captions.
- AdCreative.ai – Generate ad visuals + headlines optimized for Facebook and Instagram.

Quick Hack:
Use Pictory to turn your "About Us" page into a professional brand intro video in less than 5 minutes!

Step-by-Step: Create a Mini Campaign Using Only AI

Let's say you're launching a custom notebook business. Here's how to create a full campaign using AI:

Step 1: Logo + Branding
- **Tool:** Looka
- **Output:** Logo, brand colors, fonts, social banners

Step 2: Social Media Content
- **Tool:** Jasper AI + Canva
- **Output:** Product teaser, Instagram carousel, stories

Step 3: Email Campaign
- **Tool:** MailerLite + ChatGPT
- **Output:** Launch email, discount coupon mail

Step 4: Video Ad
- **Tool:** Lumen5
- **Output:** 30-second product showcase with music and captions

Total Time: Under 2 hours
Total Cost: 0 (free versions used)

Real-World Example: AI-Made Ad in 3 Minutes

Business: College student startup selling organic lip balms

AI Tools Used:
• **Writesonic:** For writing product benefit bullet points
• **Canva AI:** For designing ad visual
• **AdCreative.ai:** For generating multiple ad variations
• **Tome:** For making the product pitch deck

The team posted the ad on Instagram. Within 24 hours, they got 70 likes, 12 orders, and 3 collaboration offers—without spending a single rupee on hiring anyone.

AI Naming & Branding Generator

You can even brainstorm your brand identity with AI:

Sample Prompts:
• "Suggest 10 brand names for a kids' eco-toy company"
• "Design a slogan for a healthy snack bar for teenagers"
• "Generate a logo idea for a digital marketing agency run by students"

Pro Tip: Feed these prompts into ChatGPT or Looka, and see how quickly your business begins to take shape.

Consistency is Key – AI Can Help

Marketing works only if it's consistent. AI can help you:
• Schedule posts with Buffer or Canva Content Calendar
• Recycle top posts using SocialBee

• Track what's working using Metricool AI insights

Tip: Build a weekly content plan with ChatGPT + Notion AI and execute it without stress.

Should You Replace Human Creators? No – Collaborate Instead

While AI tools are fast and creative, remember:
• You set the brand tone.
• You understand your audience.
• You bring the emotion.

Use AI as your creative partner, not a full replacement.

AI + YOU = Speed + Soul

Try This: AI Branding Sprint Challenge

Total Time: 30 minutes
Goal: Build a mock campaign for a business idea

Step 1: Brand Name from ChatGPT
Step 2: Logo with Looka
Step 3: Caption with Jasper
Step 4: Design with Canva
Step 5: Video with Lumen5
Step 6: Email with MailerLite + AI

Outcome: A complete launch campaign!

Common Myths – Busted

? "AI-generated content is boring"
✓ **Truth:** You can control tone, style, and creativity with prompts.

? **"You'll get flagged for using AI in social media"**
✓ **Truth:**As long as content is original and valuable, you're good to go.

? **"Only big brands can afford AI tools"**
✓ **Truth:** Most AI tools offer free or student versions.

Reflection: What's Your Brand Voice?

Ask yourself:
- Is my brand fun or formal?
- Do I speak to teens, professionals, or parents?
- What do I want people to feel when they see my product?

Then train your AI tools to match your brand personality.

Table: Top AI Marketing Tools for Different Needs

Need	Tool	Use
Ad copy	Copy.ai, Jasper	High-conversion text for ads and landing pages
Social posts	Writesonic, ChatGPT	Quick captions, taglines, ideas
Email campaigns	MailerLite, ChatSpot	Smart automation and personalization
Branding kits	Looka, Brandmark	Logos, color schemes, fonts
Design posts	Canva, Adobe Firefly	Posters, Instagram content, flyers
Video content	Pictory, Lumen5	Reels, ads, explainers
Decks + Slides	Beautiful.ai, Tome	Startup pitch decks, reports, slides

Founder's Insight

Abeer's Take
AI can draft content, analyze audience behavior, and optimize campaigns instantly. Use it to experiment faster.
Amaara's Take
Brand trust cannot be automated. Authenticity still comes from human storytelling.

Chapter Summary

- AI makes professional marketing and branding accessible to everyone—even solo founders and students.
- You can use tools like Jasper, Canva, Looka, and Pictory to create full campaigns in minutes.
- AI helps with speed, creativity, consistency, and cost-efficiency.
- The human role is to guide the message, tone, and soul of the brand.
- Use AI to create, not imitate—your brand story still matters.

Chapter 5

Time, Task & Team Management

Run Your Business Like a Pro — Even If You're a Team of One

Introduction: The Challenge of Doing It All

Running a startup or small business is exciting—but also overwhelming.

From responding to emails and making social media posts to meeting clients and tracking orders, every entrepreneur—especially students and solopreneurs—struggles with one thing:

Time.
You've got goals, ideas, and tasks… but only 24 hours.
That's where AI-powered productivity tools come in.
In this chapter, we'll explore how AI can help you manage your time, organize your tasks, and even run teams—all without stress, chaos, or burnout.

Why Time & Task Management Is Essential in Business

Entrepreneurship is more than just having a good idea. Success depends on how well you execute.

Poor time management can lead to:
• Missed deadlines
• Unhappy customers
• Burnout
• Confusion within teams

On the other hand, structured planning makes you:
• Focused
• Productive
• Reliable
• Peaceful

And with AI, you don't need a personal assistant to get there. You just need the right tools.

How AI Helps You Manage Time Like a CEO

Let's break down how AI-powered tools act like your time coach:

Function	AI Can...
Schedule smartly	Find the best time for meetings, deep work, and breaks
Remind you intelligently	Nudge you based on task priority and your energy level
Block calendar space	Reserve "focus time" based on your habits
Optimize your day	Rearrange tasks for flow and deadlines

Top AI Time Management Tools

1. Reclaim.ai

• AI-powered calendar that syncs meetings, tasks, and habits
• Automatically blocks time for lunch, deep work, and workouts
• Adjusts your day based on priorities

Example:
Reclaim notices you've got two deadlines and reschedules a casual meeting to give you breathing space.

2. Motion

• Combines to-do list, calendar, and project management
• Rearranges your day using smart AI based on urgency and time available
• Great for freelancers, students, and agency owners

3. Clockwise

• Optimizes team meetings to reduce overlap and interruptions
• Finds focus time for all team members
• Works great with Google Calendar

Pro Tip: Use Motion to manage your personal day and Clockwise to coordinate team schedules.

AI for To-Do Lists & Task Automation

Managing tasks across sticky notes, WhatsApp, and memory doesn't work. AI can organize your day better than any diary.

ClickUp AI

• Write tasks, SOPs (standard operating procedures), and daily check-lists
• Auto-prioritize based on deadlines

Trello + Butler AI
• Visual task boards with automation
• Auto-move tasks from "To Do" to "Doing" when the due date arrives

Notion AI
• Task planner + writing assistant
• Great for students juggling multiple roles

AI for Team Management: Keep Everyone on Track

Whether it's a 2-person startup or a 10-member project team, AI can coordinate work better than a group chat.

Challenge	AI Solution
Missed tasks	Reminders, nudges via ClickUp, Notion
Unclear responsibilities	Assign owners using Trello AI + checklists
Too many meetings	Clockwise or Reclaim suggest better times
Confused team members	SOPs written by Notion AI

Use Case: A student-led nonprofit used Trello + Butler to manage tasks for a campaign launch. No one missed deadlines—even though the team was remote and working after school hours.

AI Tools for Smarter Meetings

Hate writing meeting notes? Forget what was discussed?
AI has that covered.

Fireflies.ai
• Joins your Zoom or Google Meet calls
• Transcribes the entire meeting

• Extracts highlights, tasks, and next steps

Fathom
• AI-based Zoom assistant that summarizes the call
• Sends smart summaries directly to email

Tactiq
• Captures real-time captions and creates actionable notes
• Easy for school projects and startup huddles
Impact: You can now focus on talking while AI does the note-taking.

Real Example: A Student Creator's Weekly Workflow

Name: Ayaan, 17, sells hand-drawn comic books online.
Problem: Messy workflow, missed replies, content pile-up.

His AI-powered solution:
• **Motion** – Plans his week around school + business
• **Notion AI** – Writes to-do lists + SOPs
• **Fireflies.ai** – Summarizes team brainstorms
• **ClickUp AI** – Tracks orders, shipments, and social media schedule
Result: More orders fulfilled, stress reduced, homework submitted on time!

How AI Improves Personal Productivity

Without AI	With AI
Constant context-switching	Focused blocks of time
Forgetting tasks or meetings	Smart reminders + nudges
Long, tiring planning hours	Automatic day planning
Team confusion	Clear assignments + SOPs
Time wasted on notes	Instant summaries

Activity: Design Your AI Productivity Stack

Fill this quick table:

Task	Tool I Will Try
Daily planning	
Meeting notes	
Task tracking	
Team collaboration	
Weekly reporting	

Bonus: Block 2 hours using Reclaim.ai or Motion and experience how focused your work becomes.

Time Management Prompts for ChatGPT or Notion AI

Try feeding these into your favorite AI tool:

1. "Create a weekly schedule for a student entrepreneur running an online art store."
2. "List top 10 time-wasting habits in startups and how to fix them."
3. "Make a 3-step plan to complete a school project and manage a business pitch in one week."
4. "Write a polite reminder email to a teammate about pending designs."

Work-Life Balance with AI: Yes, It's Possible

AI can also help you:

- Schedule breaks
- Plan self-care and workouts
- Say "no" to non-urgent distractions
- Reflect on your week

Use Reclaim to block 30 mins daily for a walk. Your mind matters, too.

Common Mistakes to Avoid

× Over-automating
Don't let AI schedule things that require your decision.

× Forgetting human context
Just because it fits on the calendar doesn't mean it fits in your brain. Leave breathing space.

× Not checking AI suggestions
Always review before approving AI-generated meeting times or plans.

Smart Habits to Build with AI

- Begin your day with a 5-minute AI-generated to-do list
- End your day with a reflection prompt: "What went well? What can improve?"
- Use Pomodoro-style blocks (25 mins work + 5 mins rest) suggested by AI tools
- Keep weekends light—your creativity needs recharging, too!

Chapter Summary

- AI tools like Reclaim, Motion, Notion, Trello, and Fireflies can help you manage time and tasks like a CEO.
- Use AI to plan your day, track progress, and collaborate with others—even remotely.
- Don't just work harder—work smarter with AI-powered routines.
- Consistency, clarity, and focus are the new business superpowers—and AI helps you build them.

Chapter 6

Financials, Invoices & Smart Bookkeeping

Track Your Money, Save Time & Stay Organized – The AI Way

Introduction: Managing Money Without the Stress

Ask any entrepreneur—managing money is one of the scariest and most confusing parts of running a business.

Especially when you're:

• Just starting out
• Not from a finance background
• Working solo or as a student founder

You may ask:

• "How do I create an invoice?"
• "Where did all the money go?"
• "What's my profit?"

• "How do I plan for GST or taxes?"

The good news: AI can help you stay financially smart without needing to be a math genius.

In this chapter, we'll show you how to use AI to:
• Track income and expenses
• Send invoices
• Manage budgets
• Make better financial decisions

Why AI + Finance = Game Changer for Entrepreneurs

Traditional bookkeeping and accounting require:
• Spreadsheets
• Manual calculations
• Lots of time
• Risk of errors

But with AI:
• Your expenses are auto-categorized
• Invoices are auto-generated
• Reports are auto-created
• Forecasts are data-driven

AI makes financial management simple, fast, and stress-free—perfect for busy entrepreneurs and students.

What Is AI-Based Bookkeeping?

AI-based bookkeeping refers to software tools that:
• Use automation + smart rules
• Learn from past patterns
• Suggest improvements
• Help you stay compliant

You don't need to enter everything manually. Once you set it up, the tools do most of the heavy lifting.

Top AI Tools for Financial Management

1. QuickBooks AI

- Tracks income/expenses
- Connects to bank accounts
- Creates GST-compliant invoices
- Shows profit/loss reports

Student Biz Tip: Use QuickBooks' free trial to manage your school project budget or online store income.

2. Fincent

- Modern, startup-focused AI finance tool
- Auto-categorizes expenses
- Suggests where you can save money
- Great for solo entrepreneurs and agencies

3. PromptLoop + Google Sheets

- Use AI formulas to automate spreadsheet work
- Summarize, categorize, or calculate using natural language
- Perfect for students who love Google Sheets

4. ChatPDF + AI for Financial Docs

- Upload your invoices or bank statements
- Ask questions like: "What was the highest expense?"
- AI reads and replies in seconds

Try This: Upload a sample invoice to ChatPDF and ask:
"Which line item cost the most?" – You'll get a smart answer instantly.

Creating Invoices with AI: Easy as 1-2-3

You don't need to design invoices manually in Word anymore.

Tools:
- **QuickBooks AI**
- **Zoho Invoice + Zia AI Assistant**
- **Durable Invoicing Tool**

Steps:
1. Enter client name and service/product
2. Set price and due date
3. Hit "Generate" – done!

Bonus: Some tools also send automatic payment reminders.

Smart Budget Planning with AI

Running a business means knowing:
- How much you're spending
- What your break-even point is
- How to price your product or service

AI helps by:
- Analyzing past spending
- Predicting future costs
- Suggesting budget adjustments

Example:
You tell QuickBooks: "Help me plan a 10,000 budget for my candle business."
It replies: "4,000 for raw materials, 2,000 for packaging, 1,000 for marketing…" based on industry data.

AI and Tax Readiness: No More Fear

Students and SMEs often ignore tax planning—but it matters!

With AI tools, you can:
• Track GST or VAT inputs and outputs
• Prepare reports for CA or online filing
• Stay compliant with local tax rules

Tools That Help:
• ClearTax AI Assistant
• Zoho Books + Zia AI
• QuickBooks Tax Center

Tip: Even if you don't file taxes now, practice creating a dummy tax report using sample data. It's great learning.

Real-World Example: Student Entrepreneur Using AI for Money Management

Name: Riya, 19
Business: Selling eco-friendly handmade diaries

Problems Faced:
• Forgot to track delivery expenses
• Didn't follow up on 3 unpaid invoices
• Didn't know if she was making a profit

Her AI Setup:
• **QuickBooks:** Income/Expense tracking
• **ChatGPT:** Wrote polite invoice reminders
• **PromptLoop + Sheets:** Weekly summaries
• **Notion AI:** Financial goals + monthly reports
Result: In 2 months, she recovered 4,200 in unpaid dues and improved profit margin by 15%.

How to Start AI-Powered Financial Management

You don't need everything at once. Start with one habit:

Goal	Suggested Tool
Track income and spending	QuickBooks or Fincent
Send your first invoice	Zoho Invoice or Durable
Review past expenses	ChatPDF + your bank statement
Budget your monthly spend	ChatGPT + Google Sheets
Organize receipts or bills	Notion AI or Evernote AI

Mini Activity: AI Invoice Sprint

Time: 20 minutes
Task: Create a professional invoice for a freelance gig

Step-by-step:
1. Go to Zoho Invoice (free version)
2. Enter mock client: "ABC Studios"
3. Service: "Logo Design" – 1,500
4. Due: 7 days
5. Add your name/logo
6. Export as PDF or share link

Done! You've made your first AI-generated invoice.

Prompt Ideas for Finance with ChatGPT

Try asking:
• "Help me write an invoice reminder that is polite and professional."
• "Create a budget plan for a college fest with 15,000."
• "What are common spending mistakes in new businesses?"
• "How can I price a handmade bracelet fairly?"

Mistakes to Avoid in Finance – Even with AI

× Not checking tool outputs
AI is smart—but not perfect. Review every invoice or calculation before sending.

× Mixing personal and business money
Use separate accounts or labels in your tool.

× Ignoring small expenses
They add up! AI tools help spot "leakages."

× No backup or records
Always export monthly reports and save them securely.

Compare: Manual vs AI Bookkeeping

Manual	AI-Powered
Time-consuming	Automated and fast
Risk of errors	Smart checks and auto-correction
Paper-based	Cloud-based and accessible anywhere
Requires accounting knowledge	Beginner-friendly with tips and guidance

Chapter Summary

• AI tools like QuickBooks, Fincent, PromptLoop, Zoho, and ChatPDF make financial tasks simple and fast.
• You can send invoices, track money, and plan budgets even as a student or solo founder.
• Use prompts to plan spending, write reminders, and analyze statements.

• Start with one task—like invoicing or budget tracking—and grow from there.
• Financial literacy is a superpower. With AI, it's easier than ever to build.

Founder’s Insight

Abeer’s Take
Automate repetitive tasks first — scheduling, emails, data entry. Efficiency compounds over time.
Amaara’s Take
Automation should improve customer experience, not remove the human touch completely.

Chapter 7

Customer Support & CRM with AI

Automate Conversations, Build Relationships, and Close Sales Faster

Introduction: Why Customer Support Is the Heart of Business

What's the difference between a good business and a great one?

Customer experience.
In today's digital world, customers expect fast replies, helpful answers, and a smooth buying journey. But for students, solopreneurs, and small business teams,

It's hard to:
• Respond 24/7
• Answer in multiple languages
• Follow up with every lead
• Remember customer preferences

This is where AI-powered customer support and CRM (Customer Relationship Management) tools come in.

They help you:
• Respond instantly
• Stay organized
• Convert more leads into loyal customers
• Save hours every week

Let's learn how.

What Is AI in Customer Support & CRM?

AI tools in customer service and CRM help businesses:
• Answer questions automatically
• Track customer details and conversations
• Suggest next steps (like sending offers)
• Help your sales grow—even while you sleep

You don't need to hire a full team. With smart bots, you can offer personalized, professional service at scale.

Top AI Tools for Customer Support & CRM

1. ChatSpot (by HubSpot)
• Combines CRM, chatbot, and assistant in one
• Helps you manage contacts, deals, and conversations
• Works via chat—just ask: "Show me leads from Delhi"

Best for: Solopreneurs and startups that want a CRM + chatbot combo

2. Quickchat
• AI chatbot that answers FAQs in real time
• Can be added to websites, WhatsApp, or online stores

• Trained on your website content or business docs

Try This: Add Quickchat to your online portfolio. It'll reply to visitor questions like: "Do you ship to Mumbai?"

3. Zia by Zoho
• An AI assistant inside Zoho CRM
• Suggests leads to follow up
• Detects customer mood from conversations
• Reminds you to send quotes or invoices

4. Kuki AI
• Friendly chatbot that chats like a human
• Can be trained to talk about your product, offers, or events
• Great for creative brands and D2C businesses

What Is CRM and Why Should You Use It?

CRM (Customer Relationship Management) is a tool that stores all your customer information in one place:
• Names
• Emails
• Purchases
• Conversations
• Notes and follow-ups

AI-powered CRMs take this to the next level by:
• Tracking activity
• Predicting which customer might buy again
• Recommending the best time to reach out

Think of CRM like a memory-boosting notebook for your business.

Real-World Use Case: Student Jewelry Business

Business: Arohi, 18, sells handmade jewelry on Instagram
Problem: Missed DMs, forgot to follow up, late replies

AI-Powered Solution:

- Quickchat answers FAQs like shipping, return policy
- Google Form + Zapier stores leads in a sheet
- ChatGPT writes custom follow-up messages
- Zoho CRM tracks repeat customers

Result: More trust, faster replies, and 30% repeat buyers in 2 months.

From Lead to Loyal Customer – AI in Every Step

Stage	What AI Does	Tool Examples
Discovery	Welcomes visitors with chatbots	Quickchat, ChatSpot
Qualification	Asks key questions to identify serious buyers	Typeform + AI logic, Zoho Forms
Follow-up	Sends reminders, offers, or thank you emails	Mailchimp AI, ChatGPT
Onboarding	Guides new customers step-by-step	Kuki AI, Intercom AI
Retention	Sends birthday wishes, reorder prompts	Zoho Zia, Salesforce Einstein

Sample Chatbot Script for a Handmade Soap Brand

Customer: Hi, what are your delivery charges?

AI Bot: Hello! We offer free delivery on orders above ₹499. For others, delivery is ₹49 across India. Want me to show you our bestsellers?
Customer: Yes, please.
AI Bot: Here you go [link]
Would you like me to place an order for you?

AI for Email Follow-Ups & Lead Nurturing

Most customers don't buy on the first contact. You need to follow up.

Tools That Help:
• **Mailchimp AI** – Designs and sends email sequences
• **ChatGPT** – Writes personalized follow-up messages
• **Zapier** – Triggers emails when someone fills a form

Hack: Write this prompt in ChatGPT:
"Write a follow-up email for a customer who asked about my online guitar course but hasn't replied in 5 days. Keep it friendly and professional."

Multilingual Customer Support with AI

Many Indian businesses serve regional markets. But replying in multiple languages can be tough.

Tools to Try:
• **DeepL AI + ChatGPT** – Translate and reply smartly
• **Quickchat** – Supports multiple Indian and global languages
• **Zoho Zia** – Language detection and smart replies

Example: You type in English, AI replies in Hindi or Tamil automatically based on the customer's input.

Common AI Use-Cases for Different Businesses

Business Type	AI Customer Tool	Task Automated
Coaching Classes	ChatGPT + WhatsApp Bot	Schedule, fees info, FAQs
Art Store on Instagram	Quickchat + Mailchimp	DM replies, email offers
Home Bakery	Google Form + ChatGPT	Order form, reminders, delivery tracking
Student SaaS Startup	ChatSpot + Zapier	Lead CRM, demos, onboarding guides

Benefits of AI in Customer Support & CRM

✓ **Speed:** Instant responses
✓ **Consistency:** Same tone every time
✓ **Availability:** 24/7 support, even when you're asleep
✓ **Personalization:** Custom replies based on customer behavior
✓ **Efficiency:** One bot can handle hundreds of queries at once

Challenges to Watch Out For

× **Robotic tone**
Fix: Train your bot with brand tone and use ChatGPT for friendly replies

× **Incomplete answers**
Fix: Feed your product FAQ into the bot training section

× **Ignoring human touch**

Fix: Let AI handle common tasks—jump in personally for emotional or sensitive cases

Try This: Build Your First AI Support Flow

Time: 30 minutes
Goal: Set up a basic AI chat flow

Tools: ChatGPT + Google Form

Step 1: Write sample questions customers might ask
Step 2: Use ChatGPT to write short replies
Step 3: Add a contact form link for custom queries
Step 4: Share on Instagram bio or website

✓ You now have a mini chatbot setup!

Prompts to Use with ChatGPT for CRM Tasks

• "Write a polite WhatsApp reply to a customer asking for a 10% discount."
• "Create a 3-email welcome series for my new customers."
• "Summarize all questions from this week's orders and create a FAQ page."
• "Generate names for customer loyalty tiers (basic, premium, VIP)."

Table: Tool Comparison for AI Support & CRM

Tool	Best For	Cost (Approx.)
Quickchat	Website/WhatsApp chatbots	₹0 – ₹1,000/month
ChatSpot	Free AI CRM + chatbot	Free (by HubSpot)
Zoho Zia	AI CRM assistant	Starts at ₹720/month
Kuki AI	Friendly chat interactions	Free/Custom

Mailchimp AI	Email sequences + analytics	Free up to 500 contacts
ChatGPT	Writing support replies, summaries	Free + Plus plan optional

Chapter Summary

- AI tools can automate customer conversations, track leads, and improve follow-ups.
- Chatbots, CRM assistants, and smart replies save time and improve sales.
- Tools like Quickchat, ChatSpot, Zoho Zia, and ChatGPT make it easy to scale without hiring.
- Use CRM to remember every customer, track communication, and build loyalty.
- AI makes you available 24/7—even when you're in class, asleep, or traveling.

Chapter 8

Writing, Proposals & Presentations with AI

Craft Documents, Decks, and Pitches at Lightning Speed

Introduction: Writing Is Everywhere in Business

Whether you're launching a startup or running a small business, **you'll eventually need to write and present ideas like:**

- Business proposals
- Investor pitch decks
- Product descriptions
- Internal SOPs (Standard Operating Procedures)
- Emails and letters
- Reports and project plans

But what if you're not a confident writer or don't have time?
With AI, writing becomes faster, easier, and even fun. You don't have

to start from a blank page anymore—your smart writing assistant is always ready.

In this chapter, you'll learn how AI tools can help you write like a pro and present like a leader.

How AI Transforms Writing in Business

AI-powered writing tools help by:

- Generating ideas
- Organizing thoughts
- Fixing grammar and tone
- Saving time
- Creating visuals and summaries

You give the idea or prompt, and the AI gives you a structured, polished draft in seconds.

Think of it as a digital writing partner who never gets tired or runs out of creativity.

Top AI Tools for Writing & Presentations

1. Notion AI

- Smart writing inside your Notion workspace
- Writes meeting notes, SOPs, emails, and even social captions
- Can summarize, translate, or rewrite existing text

Example Prompt:
"Write a standard operating procedure for managing customer orders in my online bakery."

2. ChatGPT

- General-purpose AI writer and idea generator
- Writes blogs, letters, product descriptions, cold emails, FAQs

• Can mimic tone, rewrite content, and create outlines

Prompt Idea:
"Write a professional proposal for a social media marketing service for small businesses."

3. Grammarly Business
• Grammar checker + tone enhancer
• Fixes spelling, clarity, and formality
• Suggests improvements in real-time

Best for: Students preparing reports or emails for clients or school competitions.

4. Microsoft 365 Copilot
• AI assistant built into Word, Excel, and PowerPoint
• Summarizes long documents, generates tables, builds slides
• Perfect for preparing school projects or investor decks

5. Tome
• AI-powered presentation tool
• Converts written content into beautiful slides
• Great for pitch decks, startup intros, or school exhibitions

Try This:

Ask ChatGPT: "Write a pitch for a mobile app that helps students find part-time jobs."
Then paste the result into Tome.app—your deck will be ready in minutes!

Writing Use-Cases for Entrepreneurs & Students

Use-Case	AI Helps You With...	Tool Examples
Business proposal	Structure, tone, persuasive copy	ChatGPT, Notion AI
Pitch deck	Slide titles, content, design	Tome, Copilot
SOPs and internal guides	Clear step-by-step instructions	Notion AI, Grammarly Biz
Customer email or reply	Professional tone and clarity	ChatGPT, Grammarly
Investor summary or business plan	Drafting concise business overviews	Microsoft Copilot, ChatGPT
Product description	SEO-friendly, benefit-focused copy	Jasper, Writesonic

Example: AI-Generated Business Proposal

Prompt to ChatGPT:
"Write a 1-page proposal for a handmade soap brand offering a Diwali gift box collection to corporate clients."

AI Output (Summary):
Dear [Client Name],
We are excited to introduce our Diwali Gift Box collection – a curated set of handmade, eco-friendly soaps perfect for corporate gifting. Each box includes 4 luxurious soaps made with natural ingredients, packed in sustainable materials with customizable branding options... Looking forward to helping you spread festive cheer!

Total time: 3 minutes
Cost: ₹0

How AI Helps in Presentations

Making a pitch deck or class presentation?

AI helps by:
• Writing slide content
• Generating visual layouts
• Suggesting graphs or examples
• Translating technical language into simple terms

Even if you're nervous about public speaking, AI can help you prepare better visuals and clearer words.

AI Pitch Deck in 15 Minutes: Try It Yourself

Goal: Make a 5-slide deck for your startup idea

Step 1: Ask ChatGPT to write a 5-slide outline
Step 2: Copy the content into Tome or Canva Presentations
Step 3: Add AI-generated visuals (use DALL·E or Canva AI)
Step 4: Practice your script with ChatGPT-generated speaker notes

✓ Done! Your first pitch deck—powered by AI.

AI in Reports and School Projects

Let's say you're making a school report on "The Future of Sustainable Packaging."

Here's what AI can do:
• Help you create an outline
• Write an introduction and conclusion
• Suggest subheadings and bullet points
• Summarize reference material from websites or PDFs
• Suggest design and layout tips

Tools to Use:
• **ChatGPT** – For content
• **Notion AI** – For formatting
• **ChatPDF** – For extracting insights from documents
• **Grammarly** – For polishing

SOPs & Documentation – AI Saves Hours

Startups and SMEs often forget to write internal guides.

But writing things like:
• “How to process a return”
• “How to onboard a new customer”
...is crucial.

Use Notion AI or ChatGPT to auto-generate SOPs.

Prompt:
“Write a step-by-step SOP for handling customer refund requests in my online store.”

Common Writing Prompts to Use with AI

• “Write a professional thank-you note to a customer who gave us a 5-star review.”
• “Summarize this 3-page report into 5 bullet points.”
• “Translate this email into Hindi.”
• “Create a slogan for a startup that sells eco-friendly notebooks.”
• “Write a formal apology letter for a delayed shipment.”

✓ Benefits of Using AI for Business Writing

Benefit	What It Means
Saves time	No need to write from scratch
Increases clarity	Removes confusion or messy grammar
Enhances professionalism	Makes small businesses look world-class
Reduces cost	No need to hire writers/design-ers
Boosts confidence	Makes students and founders feel more prepared

Writing with AI: What to Watch Out For

× **Blindly copy-pasting AI text**
✓ Always personalize and review for accuracy.

× **Using AI for sensitive or emotional messages**
✓ Human touch matters in serious conversations.

× **Overloading slides with text**
✓ Use AI to simplify, not stuff more.

Mini Exercise: AI-Powered Proposal Sprint

Time: 20–30 minutes
Goal: Create a 1-page business proposal

Steps:
1. Open ChatGPT
2. Prompt: "Write a business proposal for a weekend photography service for college students."

3. Review and edit tone
4. Use Grammarly for polishing
5. Paste into a Canva or Word template

Done! Your professional proposal is ready to pitch.

Founder's Insight

Abeer's Take
Data helps reduce guesswork. AI tools can identify trends faster than manual research.
Amaara's Take
But numbers don't capture emotions. Entrepreneurs must combine data with empathy.

Chapter Summary

• Writing proposals, SOPs, and presentations is easier with AI tools like ChatGPT, Notion AI, Tome, and Grammarly.
• You can create polished content, decks, and emails in minutes.
• Always review, personalize, and maintain your brand voice.
• Let AI assist with structure, flow, and polish—while you bring the vision, personality, and story.

Chapter 9

Research, Insights & Product Development with AI

From Idea to Innovation—Smarter, Faster, and More Informed

Introduction: Every Great Business Starts with an Idea

How do you know if your business idea is good?

What if you're building something nobody wants?

These are common fears among entrepreneurs—especially students and small business owners. But now, AI can help you test, validate, and improve your ideas before you invest time or money.

This chapter will show you how AI tools can:
- Discover trends
- Analyze competition

• Understand customer needs
• Brainstorm features
• Plan product development

Whether you're building a new product, launching a service, or improving your current offering, AI makes research and development smarter.

Why Research Matters in Business

Before launching any business or feature, you must understand:
• Who your customer is
• What they truly want
• What problems they face
• What other businesses are doing
• How your idea fits into the market

This process is called Market Research and Product Development—and with AI, it's no longer boring or slow.

Top AI Tools for Business Research & Innovation

1. Perplexity.ai
• Think of it as a super-powered search engine
• Gives short, verified answers with sources
• Great for researching market trends, competition, or ideas

Try this prompt:
"Who are the top 5 D2C skincare brands in India in 2025?"

2. DeepResearch.ai
• Helps validate startup ideas with instant data
• Generates SWOT analysis, target personas, and problem statements
• Built for students, startups, and solopreneurs

3. NotebookLM (by Google)
• AI reading assistant for your PDFs, notes, and research files
• You can upload multiple documents, and it will find answers from them
• Great for analyzing case studies, reports, or interview transcripts

4. Consensus.app
• AI tool that summarizes real scientific and market research
• Focused on evidence-backed answers
• Great for innovation-driven products or health/wellness niches

5. ChatGPT + Claude AI
• Help brainstorm ideas, features, and use-cases
• Summarize feedback
• Generate user personas, surveys, and reports

Prompt idea:
"Act like a product strategist. Help me design a basic version of an app that connects students with local tutors."

Using AI for Market Research: Step-by-Step

Let's say you want to launch a healthy snack subscription box for students.

Step 1: Understand the market
• **Use Perplexity:** "What are popular healthy snacks among teens in India?"
• **Use ChatGPT:** "What problems do students face when eating snacks during exams?"

Step 2: Study the competition
• **Use Consensus:** "Summarize research on Gen Z eating habits"
• **Use NotebookLM:** Upload marketing reports or startup case studies

Step 3: Create a user persona
• Use Claude or ChatGPT: "Create a user persona for a 17-year-old female preparing for board exams who snacks frequently."

Build a Business SWOT with AI

A SWOT analysis helps you understand your:
• Strengths
• Weaknesses
• Opportunities
• Threats

Prompt for ChatGPT:
"Create a SWOT analysis for a student-led startup selling eco-friendly school supplies."

Output:
• **Strengths:** Unique story, low cost, youth appeal
• **Weaknesses:** Limited capital, small team
• **Opportunities:** School partnerships, CSR campaigns
• **Threats:** Established stationery brands

Real-World Example: Product Innovation with AI

Business: Ishaan, 20, wanted to create an app to help parents monitor screen time for kids.

What He Did with AI:
• Used DeepResearch.ai to validate if this is a common parental problem
• Asked ChatGPT for 3 MVP (minimum viable product) versions
• Got user feedback via a Google Form and analyzed it with Claude
• Used NotebookLM to summarize parenting blogs and articles

Result: Built a working prototype in 2 weeks and got 100 early users

Using AI to Develop New Features

Already have a product or service? Use AI to:
- Gather feedback from chats, emails, or surveys
- Summarize what users want
- Prioritize feature requests
- Generate user journey maps

Prompt:
"Summarize 50 user reviews of my e-learning platform to identify what users like and what needs improvement."

AI for Brainstorming Product Ideas

You can even use AI to come up with business ideas based on trends.

Prompts to Try:
- "Suggest 10 business ideas for students using AI tools"
- "Brainstorm a product idea using waste coconut shells"
- "What side businesses can a tuition teacher start using AI?"

AI can act as your co-founder, helping you go from idea → plan → prototype.

AI for Surveys and Feedback

Use AI to:
- Write smarter questions
- Analyze responses faster
- Group answers by themes
- Visualize data

Tools to Use:
- Google Forms + AI analysis in Sheets
- Tally + ChatGPT

• Typeform + Claude summaries

Prompt:
"Analyze 20 student feedback responses and tell me 3 common problems mentioned."

Bonus: Build a Product Roadmap with AI

A product roadmap is a plan of what you'll build, when, and why.

Prompt to ChatGPT:
"Create a 3-month product roadmap for a mobile app that helps students plan their study schedule."

Output:
• **Month 1:** MVP with core feature
• **Month 2:** Feedback collection and analytics
• **Month 3:** Launch referral program and expand features

AI = Your Innovation Partner

AI isn't just for doing tasks. It's also for:
• Thinking with you
• Offering new perspectives
• Giving evidence-backed insights
• Acting as a brainstorm buddy
The more context you give, the smarter it becomes.

Watch Outs: Research with AI Isn't Perfect

× Don't trust without verifying
✓ Use sources and cross-check data from Perplexity or Consensus.

× Avoid bias
✓ Phrase prompts carefully to avoid one-sided answers.

× **Don't overbuild**
✓ Focus on MVPs. Let real users guide future features.

Mini Activity: Validate Your Idea with AI

Time: 30–45 minutes
Goal: Research and validate a business idea

Steps:

1. Choose an idea (e.g., dog-walking service for busy families)
2. Use Perplexity to check if demand exists
3. Ask ChatGPT to create a user persona and pain points
4. Build a 5-question survey with Typeform + AI
5. Use Claude to summarize responses (real or mock data)

✓ Done! Your first AI-powered market research exercise.

Chapter Summary

- AI tools help you with market research, idea validation, feature planning, and more.
- Tools like Perplexity, DeepResearch, NotebookLM, Consensus, and ChatGPT save time and boost innovation.
- Always pair AI insights with real-world testing and feedback.
- Use AI as your partner in planning, not just an assistant in execution.

Chapter 10

Automation & Workflow Magic with AI

Do Less. Achieve More. Let AI Handle the Repetitive Stuff.

Introduction: What If Your Work Could Do Itself?

Imagine this:
• A new customer fills out a form → They instantly get a welcome email.
• You upload a file → It auto-saves to Google Drive and notifies your team.
• Someone books a call → They receive a WhatsApp reminder, a meeting link, and a follow-up doc.
Magic? No—it's AI-powered automation.

In this chapter, you'll learn how to:
• Automate everyday tasks
• Connect your favorite apps

• Build smart workflows without code
• Save hours of manual work each week

Whether you're a student startup founder or a small business owner juggling multiple hats—automation will change how you work forever.

What Is Automation in Business?

Automation means using tools to do work without manual effort.

With AI, automation becomes even smarter—it:
• Triggers actions based on rules
• Connects different platforms
• Customizes workflows
• Reduces the need for reminders, copy-pasting, and admin stress

Think of it as hiring invisible interns who follow instructions perfectly, every time.

Top Tools for Automation & Workflow Management

1. Zapier
• Connects 6,000+ apps (Google Forms, Gmail, WhatsApp, Shopify, etc.)
• "If this happens → do that" logic
• Easy drag-and-drop workflow builder

Example: "If someone fills my website form → Send them a welcome email + add to Notion CRM + alert me on Slack."

2. n8n.io
• Free, open-source workflow automation tool
• More customizable than Zapier
• Great for students or devs who like building logic visually

3. AIrops

- Built for startups and digital businesses
- Automates marketing, sales, and customer success flows
- Works with CRMs, payment gateways, and forms

4. Manus.ai

- Combines AI with automation
- Reads data, decides the next step, and acts
- Example: Reads an email, identifies it's a refund request → auto-responds and initiates refund flow

What Can You Automate as a Student Entrepreneur?

Task	Automation Example
Form to CRM	"New Typeform entry → Add to Airtable or Notion CRM"
Appointment booking	"Calendly booking → Send Google Meet link + add to Calendar"
Order processing	"New order → Add to inventory sheet + send invoice via Gmail"
Follow-ups	"No response in 3 days → Send reminder email automatically"
Content scheduling	"New blog → Auto-post on Twitter and LinkedIn using Buffer"

Every time you repeat a task manually, think—can I automate this?

Real-Life Example: Student Clothing Brand

Business: Riya, 17, sells custom t-shirts
Problem: Manually messaging customers, sending confirmations, and updating Excel sheets

Automation Setup:

- Typeform for order form
- Zapier connects form to Google Sheets
- Sends confirmation email + adds to Airtable CRM
- Sends WhatsApp alert using Twilio integration

Result: Saved 2+ hours per day and reduced order mistakes

Common AI Automation Triggers

Trigger	Action Example
New form filled	Send email + store data + notify team
New email received	Auto-reply + move to folder + add task to Trello
Calendar event scheduled	Send reminder + create Zoom link + update CRM
File uploaded to Drive	Notify team + tag and organize folder
Social media comment	Auto-reply or flag for support

AI in the Workflow: It's Not Just Rules—It's Smart Rules

Traditional automation follows IF → THEN logic.

AI automation adds:

- **Context understanding** (e.g., detect tone of an email)
- **Smart suggestions** (e.g., best time to send follow-up)
- **Natural language input** (e.g., "Remind me in 2 days if no reply")
- **Dynamic behavior** (e.g., change path based on customer response)

Example: AI detects that a customer used negative words → Sends priority alert to human support.

Build Your First Smart Workflow (No Coding Needed)

Goal: Send a proposal when someone books a call

Tools:
• Calendly (for booking)
• Google Docs (proposal template)
• Zapier (automation)
• ChatGPT (personalized proposal writing)

Steps:
1. Calendly event booked
2. Zap triggers: Generate proposal with ChatGPT + Send via Gmail
3. Add contact to Airtable CRM
4. Send Slack alert to your team
Result: Personalized response, no delay, no manual work

Automation in Marketing: Set and Forget

• New subscriber → Welcome email sequence
• Website visit → Send discount popup or retargeting ad
• Inactive customer → Reminder message after 30 days
• New blog post → Share across all platforms

Tools to Use:
• Zapier + Mailchimp
• Buffer + Canva AI
• ConvertKit + ChatGPT for email writing

Tip: Start with a simple welcome email flow and build from there.

AI Automation for Business Reports

You can also automate:
• Daily sales reports

• Weekly inventory updates
• Monthly financial summaries

Use:
• PromptLoop + Sheets
• Zapier + Google Sheets + ChatGPT

Example:
"Every Sunday at 6 PM → Send a report of new orders + top-selling items + low-stock alerts."

Prompts to Use for Automation Planning

Try feeding these into ChatGPT:
• "Create a 3-step automation flow for an online course launch."
• "Write email copy for a follow-up after someone downloads my brochure."
• "Suggest 5 useful Zapier automations for a small home bakery."
• "How can I automate customer onboarding for my freelance design service?"

Watch Out for These Mistakes

× Over-automating
✓ Don't automate sensitive human communication (like apologies or conflict resolution)

× Forgetting to test
✓ Always test your flow with dummy data before going live

× Ignoring context
✓ Add filters and exceptions (e.g., don't send birthday emails twice)

Use Cases by Business Type

Business	AI Workflow Example
Art Store	New order → WhatsApp thank you → Update Airtable → Invoice
Online Course Seller	Sign-up → Welcome email → Course access → Feedback form
Coaching/Consulting	Booking → Send intake form → Reminder → Feedback request
D2C Product Brand	Abandoned cart → Reminder email + 10% discount offer

Quick Automation Challenge: 20-Minute Setup

Goal: Get an email alert every time someone fills your Google Form

Tools: Google Forms + Zapier
Steps:
1. Create a simple Google Form
2. Go to Zapier → "Google Form → Gmail"
3. Customize email text
4. Test and activate

Congrats! You've built your first workflow.

✓ Benefits of AI-Powered Automation

Benefit	Impact
Saves time	Focus on work that matters
Reduces errors	No more forgetting or repeating tasks
Boosts speed	Immediate responses and updates
Looks professional	Consistent communication and experience
Increases efficiency	Small teams can act like big companies

Founder's Insight

Abeer's Take
Transparent systems build long-term credibility. Document how your AI tools make decisions.

Amaara's Take
If your business scales but harms trust, it will collapse. Ethics is a competitive advantage.

Chapter Summary

- AI automation tools like Zapier, n8n, AIrops, and Manus help you build smart workflows.
- Automate repetitive tasks like emails, forms, reminders, and reports.
- Connect your favorite tools to work together, 24/7.
- Start small, test often, and scale what works.
- Automation gives back your most valuable resource: time.

Chapter 11

AI for Design, Video & Voice

Create Stunning Visuals, Videos & Voiceovers—No Designer or Studio Needed

Introduction: You Don't Need a Big Team to Look Professional

In today's digital world, how your brand looks and sounds matters as much as what you sell.

But design and content creation can be:
• Expensive
• Time-consuming
• Technically complex

Until now.
AI tools have changed the game.

You can now:
• Design logos and packaging
• Create explainer videos
• Record studio-like voiceovers
• Make social media reels

...all without hiring a designer, editor, or voice artist.
In this chapter, you'll explore how AI can help you bring your brand to life visually and vocally—quickly, affordably, and beautifully.

AI for Design: Make Your Brand Look Great

Even if you don't know Photoshop, you can now create:
• Logos
• Posters
• Packaging
• Social media graphics
• Website banners
• Business cards

Top Design Tools

✓ **Canva (with AI features)**
• Drag-and-drop design platform
• Smart templates, color suggestions, and AI-powered resizing
• Magic Design: Generates visual ideas from a text prompt

Example: "Design a poster for my online yoga class for teens" → Canva AI will generate 4–5 layouts instantly

✓ **Midjourney / DALL·E**
• AI art generators
• Create images from text like: "Minimalist logo of a fox with a moon"
• Great for brand identity, illustration, and packaging

✓ **Looka & Brandmark**

• Instant logo design + full brand kit (colors, fonts, icons, social banners)

• Ideal for launching fast with professional branding

Try this: Visit Looka.com, type your brand name + industry, and get a ready-made logo and visual identity in minutes.

AI for Video Creation: Tell Your Story Without Editing Software

You don't need to know video editing to make:

• Product explainers

• Instagram reels

• Testimonials

• Promo trailers

• Social stories

Top Video Tools

✓ **Lumen5**

• Turn blog posts or scripts into engaging videos

• Drag-and-drop editor with AI scene suggestions

Prompt: "Turn this paragraph about eco-friendly packaging into a 30-second video."

✓ **Runway ML**

• Video editing with AI features like background removal, motion effects

• Great for product showcase or demo videos

✓ **Pictory**

• Automatically summarizes long content into short videos

• Ideal for turning text into social-ready reels with subtitles and music

✓ **OpusClip**
• Repurposes YouTube videos into 10+ short clips
• Adds auto-captions, transitions, and smart highlights

AI for Voice: Create Studio-Like Narration at Home

Want to add voiceover to a pitch video or podcast without recording?

AI voice tools let you:
• Convert text to natural-sounding voice
• Choose accent, gender, and tone
• Save time and cost on professional recording

Top Voice Tools

✓ **ElevenLabs**
• Lifelike AI voices in multiple languages and accents
• Great for narration, audio ads, and tutorials

✓ **Murf.ai**
• Text-to-speech with pitch and emphasis control
• Ideal for training videos and explainer content

✓ **Play.ht**
• Wide selection of voice options for social media content
• Add realistic voiceovers to short videos or animations

Real-World Use Case: 1-Day Brand Launch with AI

Business: Aditya, 21, launches an online plant shop

His 1-Day AI Setup:
• **Logo:** Created using Looka
• **Website:** Built with Durable.co

• **Promo Video:** Script + visuals using Lumen5
• **Voiceover:** Generated with ElevenLabs
• **Instagram Post:** Designed in Canva AI

Outcome: Branded business launch ready in 8 hours—with no team, no coding, and 0 spent.

Build Your Own AI Video Pitch

Goal: Create a 1-minute pitch video for your startup

Step-by-Step:
1. Write a short script with ChatGPT
2. Generate visuals using Midjourney or Canva
3. Add narration using Murf.ai or ElevenLabs
4. Assemble in Lumen5 or Runway
5. Download and share!

✓ **Result:** A professional-quality video that impresses partners, customers, or investors.

Prompts for Visual & Video Content Creation

Use these with AI tools:
• "Design a packaging label for an organic tea brand"
• "Generate a flat-lay image of stationery on a wooden table"
• "Create an explainer video about how my app helps students learn faster"
• "Write a video script for a handmade candle brand's winter collection"

AI Design Tools: Comparison at a Glance

Tool	Use	Free Plan	Best For
Canva AI	Graphics, templates, posters	Yes	All-rounder design for business & school
Looka	Logo + brand kit	Yes (download costs)	Fast startup branding
Midjourney	AI-generated artwork	No (Discord access)	Illustrators, packaging, storytelling
Lumen5	Video creation from text	Yes	Social media content, YouTube videos
ElevenLabs	Voice narration from text	Yes (limited)	Product videos, pitches, tutorials
Runway ML	Video editing with AI features	Yes	Background edits, green screen, transitions

Mistakes to Avoid in Visual + Audio AI Use

× **Overcomplicating designs**
✓ Keep it clean, clear, and focused on the message.

× **Ignoring copyright for music/images**
✓ Use royalty-free assets or AI-generated content you own.

× **Using robotic voices without review**
✓ Choose voices that suit your audience and brand tone.

How AI Helps You Stay Consistent

• Brand identity across Instagram, WhatsApp, and your website
• Matching tone of voice across emails and product videos
• Cohesive visuals that reinforce your business values

Tip: Save your brand colors, fonts, and logos in tools like Canva for easy reuse.

Activity: Launch a Mock Product in 60 Minutes

Time: 1 hour
Goal: Build a brand presence for a fake product using AI

Choose a product: Example: "Study snacks for exam warriors"
Now use AI to:
• Create a name and logo (Looka)
• Make an Instagram post (Canva AI)
• Write a promo script (ChatGPT)
• Make a voiceover (Murf.ai)
• Combine into a reel (Lumen5)

✓ You now have a full content pack—without hiring anyone!

Chapter Summary

• AI lets you design logos, posters, videos, and voiceovers—even if you're not a designer.
• Tools like Canva, Midjourney, Lumen5, ElevenLabs, and Murf make content creation fast and fun.
• Use AI to launch faster, look professional, and create content consistently.
• Always review, refine, and match your brand's message and values.

Chapter 12

Building Apps & Smart Products with No Code + AI

Create, Launch, and Grow Without Writing a Single Line of Code

Introduction: You Can Build Tech Without Being a Coder

Imagine building:
• A working app
• A full website
• A customer form
• An AI-powered chatbot
...all without hiring a developer.

Sounds unbelievable? Not anymore.
Welcome to the world of No-Code tools and AI-powered product builders.

In this chapter, you'll learn how to bring your startup idea to life—fast, affordable, and without technical skills.

Whether you're a student with a brilliant idea or a small business owner ready to launch your next product, No Code + AI = Superpower.

What Is No Code + AI?

No Code tools let you build websites, apps, forms, and digital products using drag-and-drop interfaces, not programming languages.

AI then helps you:
- Design better
- Write content faster
- Automate flows
- Add intelligence to your product

Think of No Code as your builder and AI as your brain.

Top Tools to Build Apps, Sites & Products Without Code

1. Durable.co
- Builds full websites in 30 seconds
- Just enter your business type → AI writes content and picks images
- Ideal for portfolios, local services, and product launches

2. Lovable.so
- Create MVPs (Minimum Viable Products) using AI
- Build apps with onboarding flows, dashboards, and email automation
- Great for student-led startups and idea testing

3. Typeform + VideoAsk
- Smart, conversational forms with design and logic

• Use VideoAsk to send questions via video and collect video/audio/ text replies
• Perfect for feedback, lead collection, and mini interviews

4. Glide Apps
• Turn Google Sheets into mobile or web apps
• Use templates or build from scratch
• Great for event apps, directories, or inventory systems

5. ChatGPT + Harpa + Operator
• ChatGPT helps plan features, write content, and brainstorm UX
• Harpa AI scrapes data and triggers actions from webpages
• Operator (AI agent) can perform multi-step tasks like replying to customers, filing forms, or organizing files

What Can You Build as a Non-Coder?

Idea	Tools to Use
A booking website for tutors	Durable + Calendly + Mailchimp
A mobile app for a college fest	Glide + Notion + Canva AI
A lead collection quiz	Typeform + ChatGPT + Zapier
A content platform for your videos	Substack + Lumen5 + ChatGPT
A customer support agent	Operator + Quickchat + Harpa AI

Real-Life Example: Building a Feedback App Without Code

Business: Tanu, 18, wanted feedback from customers for her home-baked cake business.

What She Built:
- **Typeform:** Feedback form with rating and text
- **VideoAsk:** Customers could send selfie reviews
- **Zapier:** Auto-save responses in Notion
- **Canva AI:** Designed thank-you postcards

Result: She collected 100+ testimonials in 2 weeks and boosted trust with new buyers.

How AI Helps in No-Code Building

AI isn't just for content—it assists at every step:

Step	AI Can Help With...
Planning	Brainstorm product features, user flow, benefits
Writing	App descriptions, button texts, FAQ
Design	Color palettes, logos, layouts
Testing	Generating mock data for testing features
Launch	Promo content, ads, and landing page copy

Prompt to ChatGPT:

"Help me design a landing page for an app that tracks study hours for students."

Step-by-Step: Build a Basic App with Glide

Time: 60–90 minutes
Goal: Make a basic inventory tracker app

Steps:
1. Open Glide
2. Upload your Google Sheet (e.g., Product Name, Quantity, Price)

3. Choose a layout (list, grid, gallery)
4. Customize with brand logo + colors
5. Share the app link with your team or customers

No code. Just click, edit, launch.

Build with AI Agents: Operator + Harpa in Action

Let's say you get 20 customer emails daily asking the same 3 questions.

Setup:
• **Harpa AI:** Scans the webpage for FAQs and stores answers
• **Operator AI**: Reads the new emails, detects the topic, sends replies using templates

Bonus: Add a prompt like: "Reply kindly and ask if they need anything else."

Result: Customer queries are auto-answered. You only step in for complex ones.

Quick Build Ideas for Students & SMEs

Product	Use-Case
Pet Grooming Appointment Site	Durable + Google Calendar + ChatGPT
Freelance Portfolio	Canva + Looka + Durable
Personal Finance Tracker	Glide + Sheets + PromptLoop
Student Notes Sharing App	Notion + AI summaries + PDFgear
Event Registration Page	Typeform + Mailchimp

Mini Challenge: Build and Launch in 1 Hour

Objective: Launch a landing page for a "Study Buddy" app

Tools:
• **Durable:** AI website
• **ChatGPT:** Content
• **Canva:** Visuals
• **Tome:** Presentation deck
• **Zapier:** Connect signup to email

Outcome: A functional, branded, sign-up ready product idea—in 1 hour.

Common Mistakes to Avoid

× **Building too much, too soon**
✓ Start with an MVP (Minimum Viable Product)

× **No clear user journey**
✓ Use AI to design user flow and onboarding

× **Over-relying on templates**
✓ Customize to stand out—add brand voice and unique features

Prompts to Help You Get Started

• "Help me plan the features of an app for finding dog walkers in my city."
• "Write 5 onboarding steps for a note-taking app for students."
• "What should I include on the landing page of an eco-friendly bag brand?"
• "How can I validate my product idea before building the full app?"

✓ Benefits of Building with No Code + AI

Benefit	Why It Matters
Speed	Launch in hours, not months
Cost-saving	No need to hire developers or designers
Simplicity	Build with visual tools and drag-and-drop editors
Flexibility	Change features or content easily as your business grows
Confidence	See real results before investing more

Chapter Summary

- You can build real apps, sites, and tools using No-Code platforms and AI—no tech background needed.
- Tools like Durable, Glide, Typeform, Operator, and Harpa help you launch fast.
- AI supports with planning, writing, and automating.
- Start simple. Launch. Learn. Improve.

Final Chapter: Ethical, Legal & Smart Use of AI in Business

Use AI Like a Pro—Responsibly, Transparently, and Creatively

Introduction: Just Because You Can, Doesn't Mean You Should

AI is powerful.
It can write, design, automate, analyze, and even think—but as entrepreneurs and students, you must learn how to use it wisely.

With great power comes great responsibility.

This chapter is about using AI:
- Legally
- Ethically
- Safely
- Responsibly

It's your guide to staying professional, original, and trusted—while using AI as your co-pilot.

The Three Golden Rules of Using AI

1. Always Review the Output
AI can make mistakes. It can "hallucinate" facts. You are responsible for the final result.

2. Don't Mislead People
Be transparent if AI helped you write, design, or automate. Don't pass it off as purely human work if it's not.

3. Respect Privacy & Ownership
Don't upload private data or steal someone else's content. Follow copyright rules.

AI and the Law: What You Need to Know

Copyright & Originality
• AI-generated content may not be copyrightable in some countries.
• If you use stock images or music in AI tools, check usage rights.
• Avoid using AI to copy someone else's branding, writing, or artwork.

✓ **Best Practice:** Always edit, reword, or customize what AI gives you.

Data Privacy
• Don't enter sensitive customer or client data into AI tools unless they're GDPR/India DPDP compliant.
• Avoid uploading personal photos, IDs, passwords, or addresses.

Tip: Use anonymized data (like initials or sample names) while testing tools.

Plagiarism & Originality Tools

To ensure your content is unique:

• Use Grammarly, Quillbot, or Copyscape for checks.

• Tools like ZeroGPT detect AI-generated text—use them if schools or clients ask.

Remember: Using AI is fine, but passing off AI's work as fully yours without input can be unethical.

Ethical Use Cases vs Unethical Use Cases

Ethical Use of AI	Unethical Use of AI
Writing first drafts, then editing	Submitting AI essays with no review
Designing logo concepts for brainstorming	Copying a brand's design with AI
Using AI to explain topics	Using AI to cheat in exams or copy homework
Summarizing documents	Generating fake facts or quotes
Automating admin tasks	Spamming leads with AI-generated emails

✓ Transparency = Trust

Let your customers, classmates, or teammates know when AI is helping.

Example:

"This presentation was created using Canva and Tome with support from AI design tools."

"This email was drafted using ChatGPT and reviewed by me."

Being honest builds credibility, especially when clients or investors value originality.

The Role of Human Judgment

AI lacks:
• Empathy
• Emotional intelligence
• Cultural understanding
• Contextual decision-making

As a human entrepreneur, your job is to:
• Guide AI
• Add empathy
• Maintain values
• Set the vision
AI is the engine. You are the driver.

What to Do When AI Gets It Wrong

Signs of Bad AI Output:
• Overconfident tone for unknown facts
• Repeating phrases or vague language
• Biased, unfair, or inappropriate suggestions
• Missing important context

✓ What to Do:
• Fact-check with Google, Perplexity, or reliable sources
• Add your personal insights or experience
• Edit and simplify where needed
• Avoid publishing raw AI text

AI Ethics in Real-Life Scenarios

E-commerce Startup Example
Bad: Using AI to write fake product reviews
Good: Using AI to summarize real customer feedback for improvement

Student Entrepreneur Example
Bad: Copying a full project report from ChatGPT
Good: Using ChatGPT to brainstorm structure and then writing with your voice

Designer Example
Bad: Asking Midjourney to "copy Apple's logo in green"
Good: Asking it to "create a minimalist tech logo for a futuristic smartwatch brand"

The Future of AI and Entrepreneurs Like You

In the next few years:
• AI will be everywhere—in schools, shops, farms, factories, and homes
• Businesses that use AI smartly and ethically will lead
• Trust, creativity, and emotional intelligence will be the most valuable human traits

You have a chance to be a responsible AI pioneer. Set the example for others.

Mindset for Using AI Wisely

1. **Curious** – Explore what AI can do, but stay aware of its limits
2. **Creative** – Don't copy; create better with AI's help
3. **Critical** – Always check, question, and improve AI output
4. **Compassionate** – Respect your audience, users, and data
5. **Confident** – Use AI boldly, but never forget your human edge

Prompts for Ethical Decision-Making

Use these for self-reflection or team discussions:
• "If I saw someone using AI this way, would I trust their business?"
• "Does this content truly represent my brand values?"
• "Am I solving a real problem or just trying to 'trick' the system?"
• "What would I say if asked how this was made?"

Create an AI Ethics Checklist for Your Startup

✓ Have I reviewed the AI content before publishing?
✓ Am I honest about AI involvement?
✓ Did I respect copyright and privacy?
✓ Is this adding value—or just automation for the sake of it?
✓ Am I still making the final decision as a human?
Print it. Follow it. Share it with your team.

Final Reflection: Use AI to Become More Human, Not Less

AI isn't here to replace your ideas, your story, or your spark.

It's here to:

- Help you scale
- Help you move faster
- Help you get started when you're stuck

But only you can bring:

- Meaning
- Heart
- Empathy
- Integrity

Use AI to work smart—but always lead with human wisdom.

Founder's Insight

Abeer's Take
The smartest entrepreneurs will not replace themselves with AI — they will amplify themselves.
Amaara's Take
The future belongs to founders who ask better questions, not just those who use better tools.

Final Chapter Summary

- AI must be used ethically, legally, and transparently.
- Always review outputs and respect data, privacy, and copyright.
- Don’t mislead your customers, clients, or teachers.
- Use AI to assist—not to cheat, copy, or manipulate.
- Human creativity + AI speed = responsible innovation.
- The future belongs to trustworthy builders—like you.

Bonus Section: Master List of 100+ AI Tools for Entrepreneurs

Your Ultimate Toolkit to Work Smart, Save Time, and Build Big

This bonus chapter is your go-to reference for discovering and exploring over 100 AI tools tailored for entrepreneurs, solopreneurs, freelancers, small teams, and student startups.

Whether you're designing a logo, automating emails, creating presentations, or managing customer support, there's an AI assistant for almost everything.
To make your life easier, we've organized the tools by category, explained what each one does, and added links so you can explore them right away.

✓ How to Use This List

• Don't memorize—bookmark this chapter!
• Use it as a digital cheat sheet while working.
• Start with 1–2 tools per week.
• Always test tools to see what fits your style and budget.

General AI Assistants

Tool	Use	Link
ChatGPT	Email, writing, research, brainstorming	https://chat.openai.com
Claude AI	Advanced assistant for multi-tasking	https://claude.ai
Perplexity	Instant research with citations	https://www.perplexity.ai
Notion AI	Docs, notes, summaries, tasks	https://notion.so
QuillBot	Paraphrasing, grammar, summaries	https://quillbot.com

Marketing & Copywriting

Tool	Use	Link
Jasper AI	Ad copy, product descriptions, blogs	https://jasper.ai
Copy.ai	Sales emails, taglines, product marketing	https://copy.ai
Writesonic	Social media, e-commerce content	https://writesonic.com
Ocoya	AI + Canva for social media planning	https://ocoya.com
Bertha AI	SEO-focused content	https://bertha.ai

Design, Logos & Branding

Tool	Use	Link
Canva AI	Posters, presentations, videos	https://canva.com
Looka	AI-generated logos + brand kits	https://looka.com
Durable	Instant business websites	https://durable.co
Brandmark	Logo design, name ideas	https://brandmark.io
Designs.ai	Voice, video, and visual creator	https://designs.ai

Social Media & Ads

Tool	Use	Link
AdCreative.ai	Facebook & Google ad creatives	https://adcreative.ai
Lately AI	Social content from long-form posts	https://www.lately.ai
Flick	Hashtags + IG strategy	https://flick.tech
Pictory	Auto video generation from text	https://pictory.ai

Productivity, Notes & Planning

Tool	Use	Link
Trello + Butler	Task boards + AI rules	https://trello.com

ClickUp AI	Team planning, docs, goals	https://clickup.com
Reclaim	Smart calendar + time blocking	https://reclaim.ai
Motion	AI task scheduling	https://usemotion.com
Akiflow	Daily agenda + focus planner	https://akiflow.com

Finance, Invoices & Bookkeeping

Tool	Use	Link
QuickBooks AI	Expense tracking + reports	https://quickbooks.intuit.com
Fincent	Bookkeeping for freelancers	https://fincent.com
PromptLoop	AI in spreadsheets	https://promptloop.com
Zeni AI	Automated finance for startups	https://zeni.ai

Customer Support & CRM

Tool	Use	Link
ChatSpot	HubSpot CRM with AI	https://chatspot.ai
Quickchat	Multilingual AI chatbot for websites	https://quickchat.ai
Zia by Zoho	CRM, analytics, reports	https://zoho.com/zia
Kuki AI	Smart conversations	https://kukibot.com

Tiledesk	AI chat + human handover system	https://tiledesk.com

Docs, Proposals & Presentations

Tool	Use	Link
Tome.app	AI-powered story-telling slides	https://tome.app
Beautiful.ai	Smart decks and reports	https://beautiful.ai
Gamma.app	Auto slides and pitches	https://gamma.app
Grammarly Business	Team grammar, tone, style	https://grammarly.com
PDFgear AI	Read, extract, summarize PDFs	https://pdfgear.com

Research, Idea Validation & Learning

Tool	Use	Link
Consensus.app	Search academic research answers	https://consensus.app
NotebookLM	Organize info + AI Q&A in notes	https://notebooklm.google
Scite AI	Citation-level search	https://scite.ai
DeepResearch	Product + competitor research	https://deepresearch.xyz

Automation & Workflows

Tool	Use	Link
Zapier	Connects apps like Gmail + Sheets	https://zapier.com
n8n	Open-source workflow automation	https://n8n.io
Make.com	Visual app integration builder	https://make.com
AIrops	AI-powered end-to-end automations	https://airops.com

Video, Audio & Voice Tools

Tool	Use	Link
Synthesia	Create AI avatars & videos	https://synthesia.io
Lumen5	Turn blogs into videos	https://lumen5.com
Runway ML	Advanced AI video editor	https://runwayml.com
ElevenLabs	Voice cloning and narration	https://elevenlabs.io
OpusClip	Short reels from long videos	https://opus.pro

No-Code Builders & Forms

Tool	Use	Link
Glide Apps	Turn Google Sheets into apps	https://glideapps.com

Typeform	Smart forms, quizzes	https://typeform.com
VideoAsk	Collect video responses from users	https://videoask.com
Tally.so	Beautiful forms + logic	https://tally.so
Softr	No-code site from Airtable/Notion	https://softr.io

AI Agents, Bots & Operators

Tool	Use	Link
Operator by OpenAI	Custom agent for tasks	https://platform.ope-nai.com
Harpa AI	AI browser assistant (web scraping + automation)	https://harpa.ai
Marblism	AI bots that do tasks like humans	https://marblism.com
Lindy.ai	AI team assistant	https://lindy.ai

Final Tips for Using These Tools

• Use free trials before buying premium plans.
• Bookmark and organize your top tools.
• Set a "Tool Day" once a month to explore new platforms.
• Keep a team toolboard using Notion or Trello to track usage.
• Don't overdo it—pick what solves your real problem, not what's trendy.

Glossary

Key Terms in AI & Entrepreneurship

Term	Definition
AI (Artificial Intelligence)	Technology that enables machines to simulate human thinking and decision-making.
Automation	The use of technology to perform tasks without human intervention.
ML (Machine Learning)	A subset of AI where systems improve through data and experience.
NLP (Natural Language Processing)	AI that helps machines understand and generate human language.
Generative AI	AI that can create new content like text, images, videos, or music.
AI Agent	A system or software that performs actions to achieve specific goals using AI.
Virtual Assistant	A digital helper that performs tasks like scheduling, answering questions, etc.
Solopreneur	An entrepreneur who runs their business alone.
SME (Small & Medium Enterprise)	A business with limited employees and resources, usually locally or regionally operated.

Chatbot	A software application used to simulate conversations with human users.
CRM (Customer Relationship Management)	Tools to manage a company's interactions with customers.
Pitch Deck	A short presentation used to explain a business idea to potential investors.
Time Blocking	A time management method where specific hours are reserved for specific tasks.
AI Workflow	A step-by-step process where AI tools are used to automate routine tasks.
No-Code	Platforms that allow users to build software without writing programming code.
Plagiarism	Copying someone else's work or ideas without giving credit.
Prompt	The question or instruction you give to an AI tool to get a response.
Ethical AI Use	Using AI in a fair, responsible, and transparent way.
Freelancer	A self-employed person offering services, usually to multiple clients.
Pitch	A persuasive speech or message to sell an idea or product.

Book Summary

Your Journey with AI for Business

Welcome to the future of entrepreneurship—powered by Artificial Intelligence!

In this book, we explored how AI is revolutionizing the way entrepreneurs and SMEs operate, helping them save time, reduce costs, increase creativity, and work smarter.

Here's what you learned:

✓ **Chapter Highlights**

• **Chapter 1:** What AI is, why it matters, and how real companies like Amazon and Swiggy use it.

• **Chapter 2:** How solopreneurs and startups can level up using AI to compete with big players.

• **Chapter 3:** The world of AI assistants, chatbots, and agents that act like your digital team.

• **Chapter 4:** Creating content, ads, and branding with AI tools like Jasper, Canva, and Copy.ai.

• **Chapter 5:** Managing time, tasks, and teams using AI schedulers and project planners.

• **Chapter 6**: Tracking finances, invoices, and budgets with smart accounting tools.

• **Chapter 7:** Using AI chatbots to support and delight your customers.

• **Chapter 8:** Writing killer pitches, decks, and proposals with the help of AI.

• **Chapter 9:** Doing market research, validating ideas, and building better products.

• **Chapter 10:** Automating repetitive work using no-code workflows and Zapier-like tools.

• **Chapter 11:** Designing logos, videos, and even brand voices using AI for visual storytelling.

• **Chapter 12:** Building apps, surveys, and websites with no code + AI combo tools.

Bonus Section
We shared a curated list of 100+ AI tools, categorized for productivity, marketing, finance, design, automation, and more—your ultimate AI startup kit!

Final Chapter Takeaway
We ended with a deep dive into AI ethics, legal rules, and smart decision-making. You now know how to use AI responsibly, creatively, and transparently.

Why This Book Matters

This guide aligns with NEP 2020 and CBSE's skill-based education goals, helping students:

- Think like digital entrepreneurs
- Understand real-world applications of AI
- Build, pitch, and launch ideas responsibly
- Learn how to use modern tools with ethics and innovation

Final Message to Young Innovators

AI is your partner. But your ideas, empathy, and creativity are the true superpowers.
Use AI to amplify your voice, not replace it.

Now go ahead—dream big, build smart, and lead the future.